WORDY BIRD

Adventures in Learning

written by Angie M. Kenrick
illustrations & character development by
Richard Waskul
created by Gregory A. Bernabei

Angie Kenrick

Dedication

For all of tomorrow's leaders – those young readers of today, especially family members and friends: Anna Elizabeth, John Gregory (Jack), Evelyn Giovanna, Joseph Mario, Danica Josephine, Anna Mae, Leah Louise, Joseph Mark, Arthur Edson (Blair), James Nicholas (Jimmy), Kayden Dee, Max Anthony, Michael James (Mickey), Rachel Elizabeth, Katie Francesca, Anna Rose, Enzo Filippo, Gretchen Claira, and Heidi Josephine.

May the written word always compliment your natural strengths, and may Wordy Bird and his friends inspire leadership in all your learning adventures.

— Greg Bernabei

Published by:
EMMA Publications
P.O. Box 654
Northville, MI 48168

ISBN: 978-0-9800074-2-8

LCCN: 2009905997

Book design by Lee Lewis Walsh, Words Plus Design, www.wordsplusdesign.com

Printed in the United States of America

Meet the characters...

Wordy Bird

Long ago, Wordy Bird was walking along, minding his own business, when *PLUNK!* All of a sudden a dictionary fell from the sky and landed right on his head! Wordy Bird instantly became a "word-wiz" from this freak event. Now he uses his special gift to help students learn powerful words.

Bookworm

Bookworm is Wordy Bird's sidekick. In his mind, whatever he reads becomes real. Each time Bookworm dives into a book, he takes-off on an awesome adventure!

Buns Bunny

"The Donut-Lover"
Buns never leaves home
without his favorite snack –
donuts.

Chippy Chipmunk

"The Donut-Chaser"
Chippy would do just about
anything to sink his teeth
into a delicious donut.

Dawn Dove

"The Teacher's Pet"
Dawn is always on the edge
of her seat with her pocket
dictionary and the
correct answer.

David Dove

"The Golden Student"
David loves learning at
school, but he is often
embarrassed by his over-
bearing mother.

Sam Sparrow

"The Dreamer"
Sam is often caught
with his mind on
other things.

Ricky Raccoon

"The Class Clown"
Ricky is often caught
running with his favorite
pair of scissors.

Gary Goose

"The Quiet One"
Gary loves to sit back
and take it all in.

Freddy Fox

"The Sly Guy"
Freddy loves to play tricks
just as much as he loves
to learn.

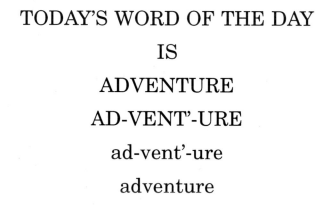

TODAY'S WORD OF THE DAY
IS
ADVENTURE
AD-VENT'-URE
ad-vent'-ure
adventure

They're here! They're finally here! thought Bookworm as he watched the boys and girls file in and take their seats.

"Good morning, eager students," said Wordy Bird in his usual start-the-day kind of way.

"Good morning, Wordy Bird," the class replied.

"Today we have something special, er, I mean, *somebody* special here to help us learn about our word-of-the-day, ADVENTURE."

Bookworm stood next to Wordy Bird with his head held high. He felt honored that Wordy Bird asked him to teach the class about ADVENTURE.

"Since Bookworm is an expert at ADVENTURES," Wordy Bird began, "he has offered to use his airmobile to take us all on an exciting ADVENTURE!"

"Hooray!" The class cheered.

"Follow me," said Bookworm. "My airmobile awaits."

Chippy grabbed Buns' box of chocolate glazed donuts, just in case his tummy grumbled along the way. Buns, with his mind on the upcoming ADVENTURE, was too excited to notice.

"AD-VENT'-URE, AD-VENT'-URE, AD-VENT'-URE!" The class sang as they all raced out to the idling airmobile.

The airmobile took off with a jerk. Buns felt the wind in his face as he looked at the ground below. Tiny trees looked just like little bunches of broccoli while the fluffy clouds whizzed past his floppy ears. "Wow! What an ADVENTURE!" cried Buns.

Sam Sparrow flew next to the airmobile. "Look," he exclaimed. "It's the crows!"

"Howdy, crows!" called Bookworm. "Can we join your formation?"

"Certainly," replied the crows. "Join in!"

Grrrooowwwlll. Just then, Chippy heard his grumbling tummy cry out for a snack. He reached into Buns' box of donuts.

The crows stared. "Yummmm! Is there enough for us?"

"Certainly," replied Chippy. "Join me for a picnic on the wing of the airmobile!"

"Wow! We've never had a picnic on the wing of an airmobile with a chipmunk!" shouted the crows. "This is quite an ADVENTURE!"

Chippy slipped Buns' box of donuts out to the wing and gave one to each of his new pals.

"This is the most delectable snack we've ever had!" said the crows. "Thank you, Chippy!"

"Don't thank me," Chippy said. "Thank Buns. They're *his* donuts."

"Thank you, Buns!" shouted the crows.

Buns turned his head. "What?" he yelled over the humming of the airmobile. Just then he noticed the picnic already in progress. "Hey! My donuts!"

"Don't worry," Chippy said. "I saved one for you too, Buns!"

WRITE ON!
Draw a picture and write about your favorite ADVENTURE.

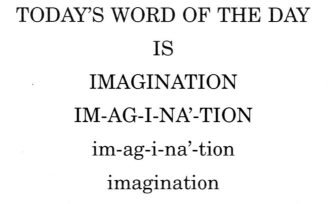

TODAY'S WORD OF THE DAY

IS

IMAGINATION

IM-AG-I-NA'-TION

im-ag-i-na'-tion

imagination

The sound of moving pencils filled the air. Wordy Bird anxiously wait-
ed for his students to draw a picture using today's word-of-the-day,
IMAGINATION.

"I'm done Wordy Bird," Dawn Dove waved her paper in the air. "Can I
show everyone my picture of IMAGINATION?"

"Sure Dawn," said Wordy Bird. "But first, do you know what IMAGINATION is?"

"Of course," Dawn replied, "IMAGINATION is the picturing power of the mind. I use mine all the time. The more you use your imagination, the more your imagination will grow."

"Great job, Dawn!" said Wordy Bird. "All of us have an imagination, right?"

"Yes, Wordy Bird," the class replied altogether.

"Now Dawn, please share your picture with us."

"I'd love to," Dawn beamed. She held up a drawing of a huge chocolate glazed donut.

Chippy's eyes widened like saucers. His mouth hung open and began to water. This was the most perfect donut Chippy had ever laid eyes on.

If I could only sink my teeth into that delicious piece of art! Chippy thought as he licked his lips.

Wordy Bird asked, "Tell us about your drawing, Dawn."

"It is a chocolate donut covered with chocolate frosting and sprinkled with chocolate covered nuts. In my IMAGINATION, it is the biggest and best donut ever made."

"BONZAI!" Chippy shouted as he flew through the air. He landed right on Dawn's desk and wildly gobbled up her perfectly, delicious-looking donut. Before anyone could stop him, the drawing had disappeared!

"Why did you eat my drawing?" Dawn whined.

"I was using my IMAGINATION to taste the biggest donut ever made," Chippy said while wiping imaginary crumbs off of his mouth.

"Well how was it?" asked Wordy Bird.

"Lip-smacking!" said Chippy. "There's only one thing that could have made it better."

"What's that?" Dawn wondered.

"Next time could you imagine a glass of milk to go with it?"

WRITE ON!
Draw a picture and write about how scientists use their IMAGINATION.

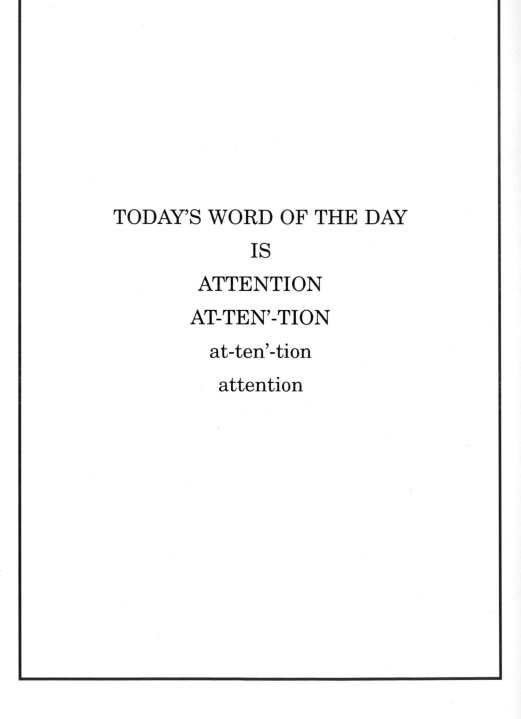

TODAY'S WORD OF THE DAY

IS

ATTENTION

AT-TEN'-TION

at-ten'-tion

attention

"Tick-tock, Mr. Sparrow," Wordy Bird said as he let out a huge sigh. "We're waiting..."

Sam Sparrow looked around at the class of staring eyes. *What's everyone waiting for?* he wondered.

David Dove covered his beak with his wing and whispered, "ATTENTION, Sam - today's word-of-the-day."

"Oh, yes. ATTENTION," Sam sat up and announced to the class.

"Nicely done, Mr. Sparrow, but where did you get your answer?" Wordy Bird questioned.

Sam Sparrow was about to tell a fib when Mama Dove hovered over and heard all the hullabaloo. She immediately swooped down, as she often did, to a perfect landing.

"Sam knew the word, because my super smart and extremely handsome son, David Dove, was paying ATTENTION!" Mama said proudly.

"Ugh! Mom!" David Dove whined with embarrassment. His face turned as red as a fire engine.

The class snickered.

"Thank you Mama Dove," said Wordy Bird. "That's a very good example of using our word-of-the-day in a sentence. Does anyone know how to spell our word-of-the-day?"

David Dove's twin sister Dawn quickly said, "I already looked it up in my little dictionary, Wordy Bird! It is spelled A-T-T-E-N-T-I-O-N, and it means 'be present, be mindful, and notice.'"

"Hooray for Dawn!" Mama Dove clapped her wings proudly. David Dove wished he could hide behind the tree.

"Thank you, Dawn," said Wordy Bird. "I know I can always count on you and your little dictionary. Now class," Wordy Bird continued, "I would like everyone to pull out a sheet of paper and..."

But before Wordy Bird could finish his directions, a loud noise came booming from the sky.

ZOOM! THUNK! "Sorry I'm late," said Bookworm while straightening his scarf. Bookworm's landings were not quite as perfect as Mama Dove's. "I met the crows on my way here. We were doing some super cool flying formations. I guess I wasn't paying attention to the time, and that's why I'm late."

"Very good!" said Wordy Bird.

"Huh?" Bookworm wondered why *not* paying attention was a good thing.

"You just used today's word-of-the-day in a sentence for us," explained Wordy Bird.

"I did?" said Bookworm. "Glad I could help, but I don't even know what the word-of-the-day is."

"It's ATTENTION," called out Sam Sparrow, "which I promise to pay more of during our classes."

"Oh," replied Bookworm. "And I promise to pay closer ATTENTION to the time. I don't want to be late for tomorrow's word-of-the-day!"

WRITE ON!
Draw a picture and write about how paying ATTENTION helps you at school.

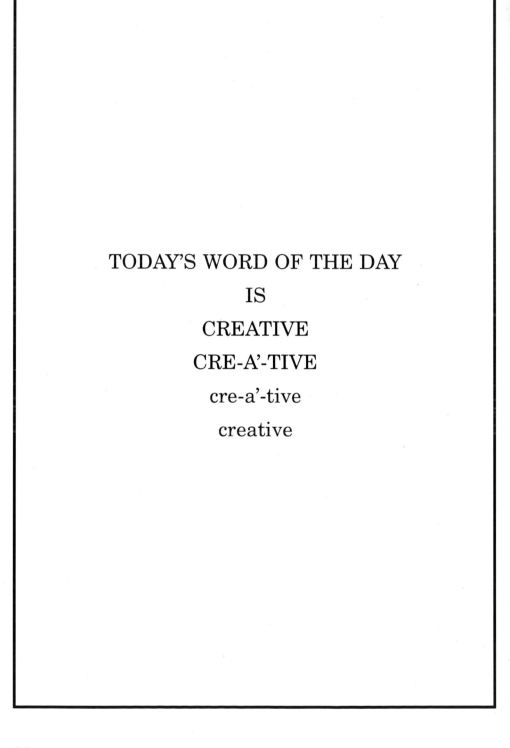

TODAY'S WORD OF THE DAY

IS

CREATIVE

CRE-A'-TIVE

cre-a'-tive

creative

Wordy Bird stared selectively at his students. "Who would like to volunteer to demonstrate today's word-of-the-day, CREATIVE?"

The students looked at each other. They thought for a few moments about what it means to be CREATIVE.

Suddenly Ricky Raccoon had a brilliant idea. He threw his hand into the air, "I'll do it!" he cried. "I will use my scissors to demonstrate the word CREATIVE in two steps."

"Two steps?" asked Sam. "I gotta see this one!"

Quickly Ricky Raccoon picked up a piece of paper and announced, "With this paper and these scissors, I will show that being CREATIVE means making something special from the ideas in your mind. The first step is thinking, the second is doing."

The class stared silently, waiting for Ricky's demonstration.

Click, click, click. Ricky Raccoon began cutting the paper wildly. Faster and faster the scissors snapped as little bits of paper flew through the air.

Wordy Bird's smile stretched out a mile, "You are doing fantastic, Ricky. When will we be able to see something CREATIVE?"

"In three, two, one, now!" Ricky said proudly.

The class gathered around Ricky Raccoon's desk as he unfolded the piece of paper. It was a picture of him, cutting out a picture of himself, holding up a donut.

"Well... what do you think?" asked Ricky.

"That is CREATIVE," said Wordy Bird. "and it shows the two steps for being CREATIVE - first thinking, and second doing."

"Awesome!" replied Dawn Dove.

"Terrific!" said Wordy Bird.

"BONZAI!" cried Chippy.

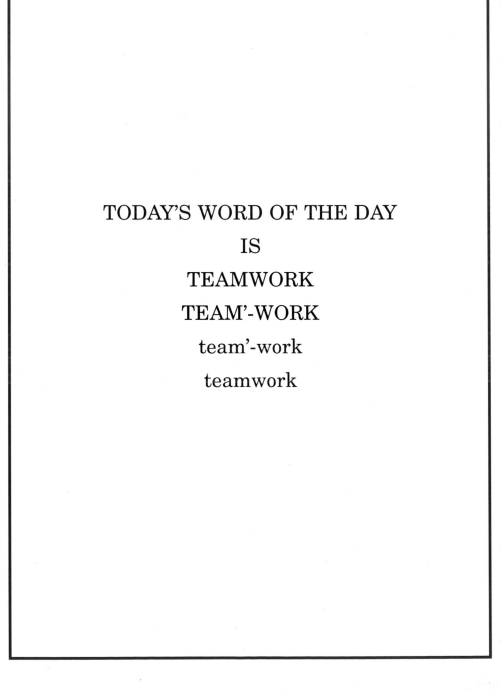

TODAY'S WORD OF THE DAY

IS

TEAMWORK

TEAM'-WORK

team'-work

teamwork

WRITE ON! You be the author.
Use this illustration to write a short story about
the word-of-the-day, TEAMWORK.